soman gouda

seedlings of light

a haiku collection

Soman Gouda

Soman Gouda is a writer, filmmaker and poet from India. His debut fiction in Kannada 'Gulabi Kode' a short story collection was well received by the readers with rave reviews. His enduring fascination with the films and spirituality inspired his first non-fiction work 'Yogi in Suits', which came into limelight in a very short span of time and garnered international acclaim.

Soman admires Gibran, Rumi and Tagore's poetry, 'seedlings of light' is his first haiku collection. His debut feature film 'Mocktale' received a great response and appreciation from the audience. He is an emerging creator of art from India with maverick perspectives and genuine insights.

soman gouda

seedlings of light

a haiku collection

SomeKranthi Creations
Bengaluru, India

SomeKranthi©
India

Published by SomeKranthi Creations
16/2, 3rd Floor, Muniswamappa Road, Halasuru,
Bangalore 560008, Karnataka,India
Mob: 9985007590
somekranthi@gmail.com

Copyright © Soman Gouda
First Print : 2019
ISBN : 978-81-937272-3-2
Pages : xii + 148 = 160
Used Paper : 70 GSM Book Print
Book Size : 12.85 cm * 19.84 cm
Book designed by Sudena

The views and opinions expressed in this are the author's own and
are as reported by him which have been verified to extent possible,
and the publishers are not in any way liable for the same.

Typeset in Bookman Old Style by Lakshmi Mudranalaya, Bengaluru

To all the secret poets
and the first lines in their personal diaries

PREFACE

many took the leap
with the frog, only to become Basho's
ignoring the frog and pond

In all the great literature, be it prose or poetry, there are few lines and verses, that make the opus sublime. Poet is possessed and in a state of trance while those rare lyrics are produced, he is a mere vehicle to the flow of divinely creation and expression. Such state of elevation doesn't last longer even if the wordsmith desires. It ends like a dream. This is the reason, that all the verses of Shelly are not equally noteworthy, so are Rumi's. Authors meditate on this immersion to create their *tour de force.*

In the contrary, a haiku is a momentary revealation, it is sculpting the miracle in time with the realtime quotidian experiences.Precisely, an interplay between the perception and intuition.Literary world has kept on witnessing a proliferation of writings in this genre of poetry due to its simplicity, compact nature and accessibility. Haikus can be written and read by anyone, anywhere in the time of need and joy.

i don't know who proposed first
all that I remember is her smile and his shyness
says love

I am not sure yet, if it's me who pursued haiku or its haiku that came to my door, love happens in a mysterious way. It was Basho, Issa and Jack Kerouac who invited me to this euphoria. Zen life has always been my fancy, so I suspect that, my heart found Haiku as an alibi and a way for it. I am grateful to those Japanese crows, butterflies, cherry blossoms, herons, mountains, horses, ponds, temple bells, frogs and rice fields for inspiring numerous poets. There are no more ancient ponds but the perceiver is still the same. We have subways,gulmohars, traffic signals, elevators, mangoes, umbrellas, bow ties, rain drops, sparrows, feathers, clouds, pot vines, love, loneliness, art, irony, time, death and so on. All that we need is a path for the heart to love and appreciate life and live it to the fullest. Haikus are the flowers on that path.

'seedlings of light' is an outcome of my tryst with the magical moments, daily experiences and zen aspirations. There are 151 haikus in this book, that are written over the course of an year. Traditional haikus capture the imagery and when they go through evolution, they capture the thoughts like an imagery, this collection consists of both the types.

they make love
in the sculptures
on a temple wall

Haikus aren't classified based on any category. They are ordered in a way that our mind works and the way they occured to the writer. If time is horizontal axis, vertical will be the heterogeneity in mind. We are driven by wide variety of thoughts in any given point of time, for example, one could think of making love while in the temple for worship!. From morning to evening, we think of almost everything about life but never in an order, and hence, expecting the unexpected is always a thrill, building and demolishing a sand castle is always a joy.

Soman Gouda
2019, July

a broken mirror

tries hard to fix itself

everytime she smiles at it

tamarind seedling

on a cowdung cake -

green phoenix

tree leaning over the stream

offers its leaves

without asking their consent

footsie with an unknown

in a pilgrimage bus -

enlightenment

funeral of flowers

over and inside the coffin

sun dips into the sea

without making him wet

sea washes

fisherman's soul

6

creeper in my office

wears a fancy tie occasionally -

yellow and red leaf

ant on my table

suddenly thinks about traffic on road -

rebirth

wind chimes

deliberate on dhamma -

chipmonk meditates under a bodhi leaf

rival writers

laid one over the other

in the shelf of an old book shop

pen bleeds in pocket

scared !

of the ghost story its about to write

who am i ?

i asked mirror -

a shooting star fell from sky

i flew over bangalore

as a sparrow in spring -

god signed his painting

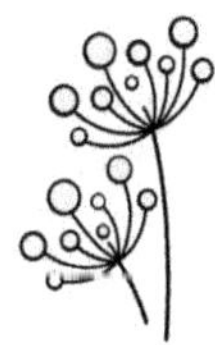

bucket overflows

president's face is wet

in the newspaper

a lonely postbox

sings lullaby to the phone booth -

public melancholy

i fight the time

in life and death

just to lose with dignity

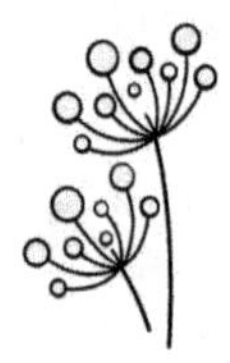

grass meditates

with the beads of dew -

squirrel prefers fresh

every kiss of her

unclasps my wings and ignites the intuition -

first rain of monsoon

butterfly sits on my table

asks me to paint her

flew away when i begin

half of the sweetness in mango

is instilled by her

while she chooses it for me

i went in search of the cloud

that kissed my mountain

i found kisses everywhere but not the cloud

vine in a hanging pot

grows downwards

thinking its roots are underground

neither the tree

nor the leaf

wanted to seperate

flames dance

for the rythm of her soul

on the funeral pyre

even the shadows turn colorful

when you choose the path of rainbow -

life of an artist

unmarried florist offered

the leftovers on the feet of god

while leaving...

a lonely sock on terrace hangs itself

grieving for its missing pair

it rains

cookie melts into the milk

while i wait for a haiku

tasty drink by the time

meditation

in traffic signal

by the statue of a saint

they talked of morals

over a milk coffee -

ambaaa! calf bleat heard from backyard

stirring my coffee

i uttered "cosmic phenomena!"

mom asks, if sugar isn't enough

its a haiku about

death of a tree

on the paper

foxes marry under rainbow

odour of cardmom flavoured pancakes -

my childhood

dry flowers, yellow leaves

and cigarettes butts

die again under car wheel

coffee gets even hotter

by their conversation -

tryst with the lips

all those days

when i hid under my blanket

i killed many poems with tears

they saved a kitten

on a stormy night

to leave it far away the next morning

someday i want to bloom

in your garden as your favourite flower

and make you smile everyday

the true artist

is the the truth in him

says the true artist

i am an exorcist while writing...

expel many spirits and confine them in words

only to get possessed again

there are seedlings of light

sprouting in my mind

by the virtue of seeds sown centuries ago

cottony clouds

wipe the wet moon after a long rainstorm -

crickets awake and quiet under the ivy vines

a butcher is busy

planting the trees post retirement -

renovation of a cemetery

eye lashes of a boy in remand home

become wings

while he dreams of becoming a pilot

a fresh mango seedling

wears the grace and chastity

that surrenders me to the creator

i am an incomplete poem

fixing my rhymes and rhythms

searching my poet

a haiku died

before it's born

in its first line

my heart dips into honey

everytime i remember

our moments in that far away misty moor

they smile to each other from different shores

never bothered to understand

if its the current or love flowing between them

eagle flew

through a blackhole -

a tattoo on my wrist

zen is a poem

between

these lines

there is a sound

for the blood flowing in my veins

it resembles that of photosynthesis

he can draw the tree

exactly the way it is

but she prefers original

words create

meaningful pauses -

to make us experience the stillness in life

a cat family

migrate to a quiet home in night

to discuss about the tv serials they watched

when HE goes

after the ART

it completes his HEART

i hide in these lines

like a baby kangaroo

in your heart when you read and jump

he left his HOME to find a guru

he left his guru to earn followers

god waited for him at his HOME

you are an itch in my mind

the more i scrape the more you give pleasure

but for how long? asked the abrasion

light beam

passing through my spine

illumined her eyes

she is a candle

upsidedown

with the flame of love

they demolish the cafe

where we met for the first time

they couldn't touch the tree as it's soaring high

gulmohar falls one by one

on a wet road -

tapestry of god

slippers paint my trouser bottoms

with the monsoon theme

while we walk under an umbrella

if I speak, there is a reason

if I don't, there are more reasons -

a broken radio

in a quiet zen monastery

silence echoes

statue of buddha smiles by the incense

interplay between the I's and eyes

an absurd obsession -

few call it poetry

life is walking with a

hot tea cup -

balancing is the art

i thought i am narcissist

when i loved myself deeply

now i realise it was a preparation to meet you

please close your petals

if I die in your arms -

reveries of a butterfly

lines agitate

in the grave of my mind

few escape as a breeze in moonlight

melancholy of loneliness

cleansed away by the evening drizzle

yellow leaf echoes me

i try to listen to the symphony

from the qwerty keyboard

muddy and stuck keys

neighbours quarrel

creepers hug and offer flowers to each other

breaking the border rules

deaf are those

who can't hear the rendezvous

of waves and the moon

pestle stick sprouts green

while my granny sings

her childhood folksongs

neither the butterfly nor the flower

force each other to change or exchange colours

but the fragrance and love

tired camels

running towards an utopian oasis -

modern cities

footprint

on the moon

in a pond

writing is getting yourself nude

designing your own costume

and gifting it to the world

buddha in a crowd

blooms detached -

a lotus in the pond

feather on the stairs

crawls down

step by step

my gentle teeth

save many watermelons

while eating them

wet kurchiff in my pocket

with black flowers on white stripes -

umbrellas cross traffic signal

cat teaches her kids

hide and 'seek' in moonlight -

zen master

there is always a confusion

that whether i am in confusion

or out of it

she felt like a worm

on fisherman's hook

on the day of her marriage

flower petals strewn

in the market road this evening -

spasmodic reminiscences

my grandfather made children

father built a house

and i wrote haikus

glass needs to be filled

to understand the emptiness -

zen monk on a motorcycle

a lotus pond

took fifty years to become a dumpyard -

life of modern man

i exist in your presence

and it's only you...

in your absence

good that i forgot those lines

before writing down

unfaithful ones

zen monk smiles

jasmine blooms

watching the mischief of squirrel

a child with the bun hairstyle in a metro

reminds me of buddha

ready to escape from family with h1b visa

long ago i cried when i lost

my first branded shoe

now i cry remembering that innocent boy

bow tie becomes a butterfly

while she kisses me

on neck

painting half done

cries to become complete

while the painter goes on a pilgrimage

dry mango seeds by roadside

wait for the monsoon

to go through their resurrection

i wait for her

with a bunch of lillies

and its no more a wait

this migrant bird

doesnt know to sing or build a nest

from north korea

landslide in himalayas

a drop of my sweat

glides down on her breast

flower on lapel

smells prestige

close to the heart yet lifelesss

morning dew drop

glides and slips from the vine leaf

into my coffee cup

they change pen and paper

in a hope to write different stories -

democracy

all happens

as if it's well planned !

even this haiku

intersection of the palm lines

in our last handshake is a sign

that our paths cross again

she argued

he slapped

and the ring lost

"silence please"

read the board

i flipped it and walked away

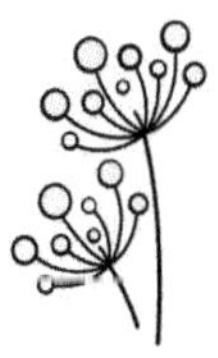

she was slept

i kissed her on the forehead

calendars flipped at my desk

a goat calls me

from window of a mutton stall

i hurried to office

cat jumped

onto a broken violin -

empty page in my diary

dry sand

in my pocket

wet again

i am a popping corn

popped up by the heat of earth

my kins waited and sprouted

a lonely bench

in a hot summer park -

couple kissed under umbrella

fallen hair, white and black

ideas sprout

between the scissors

grandpa's horse

in a vintage photograph -

an old banyan tree

succulent mango

whom to credit the sweetness

the tree, the god, or my tongue

she watched

foreign horror films -

can ghosts visit her without visa

morning and the evening

she waits at the village railway station -

silver vines entangle the porch railings

my shadow walks

when i am asleep

i am its dream

all they see is my shirt and its pocket

jasmines in their compound

go even deeper and open my heart

rain drop slips into her belly button

to become a pearl -

a monsoon evening in church street

walked home thinking hot or cold

for the night shower

it rains and i keep thinking

lensman boasts for an image of a lilly

that blooms in the wild

unaware of its royalty

furrows on her face

tell the stories

of dream harvest

broken bangles

at a court gate -

pigeon plucked a copper pod bud

never

alone

in the lift

sky is always blue

for a zen monk

as he is the cloud of wisdom

flashes

of lightning -

god walks on a red carpet

all my egos burn into ashes

by your graceful smile

after every silly argument

i breath and my clock ticks

i know i am alive

in your dreams

line of ants

in an empty coffee cup -

nazi army

every time i forget the umbrella

i remember you

wet in your memories if not the rain

i try to find name of flower

by its fragrance

google fails

you need not run a long way

just to understand its a rat race -

rat with the name Plato

you are a stranger

everyday

in a metropolis

gulmohar avenue

from the sky train -

her swaying red dupatta

a pious king sees shiva

in his woman's nipple

temple queues kept growing

i wiped the dust off an old book

and the book wiped my mind

page by page

sun is male, moon is female

its not the gender but gentleness -

musings of a moongazer

scars on my back

white trails of jet in the skies

fade away in the glory of his rays

childhood portrait

fell down on my head

disturbing my first shave

great epics might sound absurd

to some people

and you might be that great epic

global warming is a conspiracy

by all the trees to build their empire -

nightmare of an environmentalist

all the rain drops

promise to the clouds

that they go back home clean

scent of lemon leaves

in an early morning train -

a missing girl poster

three petalled flowers

an offering to thee -

a haiku